# ANCIENT ROME
## 2nd Grade History Book
## Children's Ancient History Edition

SPEEDY
PUBLISHING

Speedy Publishing LLC
40 E. Main St. #1156
Newark, DE 19711
www.speedypublishing.com

Ancient Rome was an Italic civilization that began on the Italian Peninsula as early as the 8th century BC.

Ancient Rome was a powerful and important civilization that ruled much of Europe for nearly 1000 years.

Much of Ancient Rome's history has had a lingering effect on our world today, and our citizens have learned much from their way of life.

In the early 6th Century B.C., Rome first grew into power as a Republic. The Rome leaders were elected officials that served for a limited amount of time. They had a complex government with written laws, a constitution, and a balance of powers.

In 45 BC Julius Caesar took over the Roman Republic and made himself the supreme dictator. A few years later, Caesar Augustus became the first Roman Emperor and this was the start of the Roman Empire.

The city of Rome
was the capital city
of the civilization
of Ancient Rome.

The center of Rome had many other famous and important buildings like the Colosseum, the Pantheon, and Pompey's Theatre.

The Colosseum is an oval amphitheatre in the centre of the city of Rome, Italy. It was built during the Roman Empire. Construction on the Colosseum began under the emperor Vespasian in 72 AD, and was completed in 80 AD.

It was used for gladiatorial contests and public spectacles such as mock sea battles, animal hunts, executions, re-enactments of famous battles, and dramas based on Classical mythology.

Every Roman city had a public bath where people came to bathe and socialize. Men and women bathed at different times or in different areas of the baths.

The floors of the baths were heated by a Roman system called a hypocaust that circulated hot air under the floors.

The Pantheon was originally built as a temple to the gods of Ancient Rome. The Pantheon is the best preserved of all Roman buildings.

The Pantheon's dome is still the world's largest unreinforced concrete dome. The Pantheon is the oldest standing domed structure in Rome.

While Rome was the center of the empire, there were many large and important cities throughout the empire. The most important area of every Roman city was the forum.

The forum was a
gathering place of
great social significance,
and often the scene
of diverse activities,
including political
discussions and debates,
rendezvous and meetings.

The Romans are famous for keeping lots of written records. It was how they kept their large empire organized.

They kept records on every Roman citizen. They also kept written records of laws and decrees made by the government.

M·FIL·SEVE

CO·PONTI

IL·ANTON

O·P·TIMI

ESTITVI

RO PIO PER
IC MAXIM
INO AVG I
S FORTISS
AM IMPE

Pompeii was an ancient Roman town-city. The town was founded around the 6th-7th century BC by the Osci or Oscans.

In 79 AD, disaster struck the city when it was buried under 20 feet of ash and debris from the eruption of the nearby volcano, Mount Vesuvius.

Made in the USA
Las Vegas, NV
31 July 2021

27296663R20026